Contents

Introduction

Audience and Intention

The ISTE Standards for Educators: Computational Thinking Competencies (CT Competencies) were created to inspire every educator to add more computational thinking (CT) into their core problem-solving strategies. While this resource was designed for educators, adding CT to lessons can also build students' skills and confidence in solving complex problems using computation, persisting when unexpected obstacles arise in their learning and deepening their learning in academic disciplines. Don't worry if you aren't sure you know what computational thinking is and how we use it every day—we'll get to that soon!

Many educators are already doing powerful work to integrate CT across disciplines to help students learn, use and apply computer science (CS) concepts and CT practices in different contexts. ISTE seeks to help educators recognize where this work is already happening, identify opportunities to make these connections more explicit and develop new ways to deepen student learning.

The competencies in this guide are not intended to limit classroom practices nor encourage conformity among subjects. On the contrary, the benchmarks that we introduce in this booklet provide a framework and structure to build more creative learning opportunities. We believe that increasing exposure to CT in the classroom will also increase students' ability to adapt to unfamiliar challenges, allowing for more success with innovative lesson plans.

Even if you are not already familiar with the format of ISTE Standards for Educators, this booklet will help prepare you to digest the CT Competencies in a way that allows you to visualize using them in your classroom, no matter what subject you teach.

Computer Science and Computational Thinking Explained

The CT Competencies from ISTE are part of a larger picture of preparing all students for success in a world where computing power underpins every aspect of the systems we encounter in our daily lives. They are meant to complement other CS learning frameworks, such as the Computer Science Teachers Association (CSTA) K–12 Computer Science Standards and the K–12 CS Framework. Helping educators understand what computer science and computational thinking are, how they interact and why they matter across disciplines is the foundation of this booklet.

What Is Computer Science?

In a world increasingly influenced by technology, computer science can serve as a tool for learning and expression across disciplines. Vital foundations of CS are now being introduced to children as young as kindergarten. As a result, many educators have at least an introductory understanding of what CS is, whether or not they feel comfortable defining it. In this guide, we define it like this:

> **CS is the study of computers and algorithmic processes, including their principles, their hardware and software designs, their implementation, and their impact on society.**
>
> [ACM, 2006]

Let's break that definition down.

The study of computers and algorithmic processes

This refers to learning about the machine itself, as well as the step-by-step instructions that allow the computer to do what it does. Almost all CS subjects fit into one of those two categories, where "computers" contain all of the hardware elements, and "algorithmic processes" contain everything about the creation and theory behind the software.

including their principles, their hardware and software designs, their implementation

This segment digs deeper into the important components that make up computers and algorithmic processes. The "principles" are the ideas and beliefs behind the creation of the hardware and software. Why are things made the way they are? What models have been proven to work?

"Hardware" designs include planning the inner workings of things like the motherboard, the central processing unit (CPU) and the components that store data. Physical design is a valid track of computer science and one that is mostly separate from programming.

"Software" design also focuses less on coding and more on the overall structure of the creation of a game or application. This is a critical element of computer science because it provides the overall plan and structure for what the programs will become.

Finally, the "implementation" of both the hardware and software are included. These segments, especially engineering and programming, are generally what people think of when they hear the term "computer science."

and their impact on society

The last portion of this definition is one of the most important but also one of the most overlooked. Societal impact includes topics like responsible computing, digital citizenship, data collection and analysis, as well as the expectation of ethical delivery and use, particularly as it relates to equity and accessibility.

Did you notice that the definition didn't include anything about actually using computers or software? That's because the ability to use a computer as a tool is no more a part of computer science than driving a car is part of being an auto mechanic. You're likely to use a computer while learning CS, but that use alone doesn't provide enough of a view into the inner workings to consider it a step toward understanding the overall craft. Just like driving a car doesn't give you all of the skills you need to build or repair one.

What Is Computational Thinking?

There is, of course, a lot more required of a computer scientist than just studying computers and algorithms. Computer science encourages the development of skills, practices and techniques that help when trying to figure out unfamiliar problems. One of the most important examples of this is computational thinking.

Computational thinking is not its own subject. Instead, it's a term used to identify techniques that can help solve many of the types of challenges that appear when working with technology or dealing with complex or ambiguous problems. Perhaps most confusing is the fact that the definition of CT sometimes changes, depending on the context of the discussion.

Back in 2006, Jeannette M. Wing, consulting professor of computer science at Carnegie Mellon University, brought the idea of computational thinking into mainstream K–12 education using four pillars:

1. **Decomposition.** Breaking large problems into smaller, more manageable ones.

2. **Pattern recognition.** Finding and/or matching problems or trends in data that are similar with the hope that a solution to one will lead to a solution for another.

3. **Abstraction.** Hiding the less important details of a problem or challenge to find a general solution that can later be tailored for specific instances.

4. **Algorithms.** Creating a problem-solving process composed of specific steps that can be followed for future similar problems.

Since then, researchers and educators have modified the definition of CT using what they believe to be more detailed key components to help K–12 educators put these ideas into practice. In 2011, ISTE and CSTA collaborated with leaders to create an operational definition of CT for K–12 that includes:

- Formulating problems in a way that enables us to use a computer and other tools to help solve them.

- Logically organizing and analyzing data.

- Representing data through abstractions such as models and simulations.

- Automating solutions through algorithmic thinking (a series of ordered steps).

- Identifying, analyzing and implementing possible solutions with the goal of achieving the most efficient and effective combination of steps and resources.

- Generalizing and transferring this problem-solving process to a wide variety of problems.

This reorganization changes CT from an ordered list of problem-solving tools to a set of components that make up a problem-solving process. Both are valuable, but each has its own purpose. You can expect to continue to see CT used in these different ways, depending on the situation.

This guide and the CT Competencies focus on the latter definition, where CT is a powerful ingredient for solving open-ended problems by drawing on principles and practices central to computer science in a way that can drive deeper learning across all subjects.

ISTE Standards for Educators: Computational Thinking Competencies

Preamble

> Check out the full preamble in the ISTE Standards for Educators: Computational Thinking Competencies.

Leaders and educators around the world have the enormous responsibility of preparing all students to harness the power of computing to succeed in their personal, academic or professional lives. This is an ambitious goal; the **ISTE Standards for Educators: Computational Thinking Competencies** (iste.org/standards/computational-thinking) are intended to help all educators contribute to making that goal a reality.

The ISTE CT Competencies identify the knowledge, skills and mindsets that educators need to integrate computational thinking across K–12 content areas and with students of every age. These competencies augment and home in on the competencies embedded in the ISTE Standards for Students and the ISTE Standards for Educators.

CT is at the core of computer science and a gateway to sparking student interest and confidence in learning computer science. Similar to how technology is used by educators to deepen academic learning while building digital learning skills, teachers can integrate CT practices in their instruction to introduce computational ideas. This can enhance student content knowledge and build confidence and competence in CT. By integrating computational thinking into the classroom, educators can support students to develop problem-solving and critical-thinking skills, and empower them as CS learners and computational thinkers.

ISTE recognizes that the CS concepts framed in current standards and frameworks are not only new to many students but many educators as well. Standard 1. Computational Thinking (Learner) is intended to be the beginning of a journey to understanding CT and provide a road map to support educators as they identify strengths and weaknesses, and seek out professional development opportunities to increase their mastery.

The CT Competencies present opportunities for growth and goal-setting for all educators. Whether you teach kindergarten, fifth-grade math, or 10th-grade social studies, you can leverage the CT Competencies to stretch your teaching practice.

Competency Statements and Indicators

1. Computational Thinking (Learner)

Educators continually improve their practice by developing an understanding of computational thinking and its application as a cross-curricular skill. Educators develop a working knowledge of core components of computational thinking: decomposition; gathering and analyzing data; abstraction; algorithm design; and how computing impacts people and society. Educators:

a. Set professional learning goals to explore and apply teaching strategies for integrating CT practices into learning activities in ways that enhance student learning of both the academic discipline and CS concepts.

b. Learn to recognize where and how computation can be used to enrich data or content to solve discipline-specific problems and be able to connect these opportunities to foundational CT practices and CS concepts.

c. Leverage CT and CS experts, resources and professional learning networks to continuously improve practice integrating CT across content areas.

d. Develop resilience and perseverance when approaching CS and CT learning experiences, build comfort with ambiguity and open-ended problems, and see failure as an opportunity to learn and innovate.

e. Recognize how computing and society interact to create opportunities, inequities, responsibilities and threats for individuals and organizations.

2. Equity Leader (Leader)

All students and educators have the ability to be computational thinkers and CS learners. Educators proactively counter stereotypes that exclude students from opportunities to excel in computing and foster an inclusive and diverse classroom culture that incorporates and values unique perspectives; builds student self-efficacy and confidence around computing; addresses varying needs and strengths; and addresses bias in interactions, design and development methods. Educators:

a. Nurture a confident, competent and positive identity around computing for every student.

b. Construct and implement culturally relevant learning activities that address a diverse range of ethical, social and cultural perspectives on computing and highlight computing achievements from diverse role models and teams.

c. Choose teaching approaches that help to foster an inclusive computing culture, avoid stereotype threat and equitably engage all students.

d. Assess and manage classroom culture to drive equitable student participation, address exclusionary dynamics and counter implicit bias.

e. Communicate with students, parents and leaders about the impacts of computing in our world and across diverse roles and professional life, and why these skills are essential for all students.

3. Collaborating Around Computing (Collaborator)

Effective collaboration around computing requires educators to incorporate diverse perspectives and unique skills when developing student learning opportunities. Educators must recognize that collaboration skills must be explicitly taught in order to lead to better outcomes than individuals working independently. Educators work together to select tools and design activities and environments that facilitate these collaborations and outcomes. Educators:

a. Model and learn with students how to formulate computational solutions to problems and how to give and receive actionable feedback.

b. Apply effective teaching strategies to support student collaboration around computing, including pair programming, working in varying team roles, equitable workload distribution and project management.

c. Plan collaboratively with other educators to create learning activities that cross disciplines to strengthen student understanding of CT and CS concepts and transfer application of knowledge in new contexts.

4. Creativity and Design (Designer)

Computational thinking skills can empower students to create computational artifacts that showcase personal expression. Educators recognize that design and creativity can encourage a growth mindset, and they work to create meaningful CS learning experiences and environments that inspire students to build their skills and confidence around computing in ways that reflect their interests and experiences. Educators:

a. Design CT activities where data can be obtained, analyzed and represented to support problem-solving and learning in other content areas.

b. Design authentic learning activities that ask students to leverage a design process to solve problems with awareness of technical and human constraints and defend their design choices.

c. Guide students on the importance of diverse perspectives and human-centered design in developing computational artifacts with broad accessibility and usability.

d. Create CS and CT learning environments that value and encourage varied viewpoints, student agency, creativity, engagement, joy and fun.

5. Integrating Computational Thinking (Facilitator)

Educators facilitate learning by integrating computational thinking practices into the classroom. Since computational thinking is a foundational skill, educators develop every student's ability to recognize opportunities to apply computational thinking in their environment. Educators:

a. Evaluate and use CS and CT curricula, resources and tools that account for learner variability to meet the needs of all students.

b. Empower students to select personally meaningful computational projects.

c. Use a variety of instructional approaches to help students frame problems in ways that can be represented as computational steps or algorithms to be performed by a computer.

d. Establish criteria for evaluating CT practices and content learning that use a variety of formative and alternative assessments to enable students to demonstrate their understanding of age-appropriate CS and CT vocabulary, practices and concepts.

Integrating Standards Across the Curriculum

Finding CT Opportunities in Existing Lessons

With a little forethought, CT Competencies can help educators enrich any lesson on any topic without changing the main focus of the day. In fact, the competencies are versatile and ubiquitous enough to lend themselves even to subjects that don't seem to link up with computer science or computational thinking.

In the section that follows, we'll pull multiple lessons from across the K–12 pathway and give examples of how teachers might incorporate the CT Competencies into their planning to enhance the learning experience for their students. These case studies provide general ideas for adaptations but are not intended to be complete lesson plans.

As you read through the scenarios, ISTE has bolded the concepts that the example addresses. Note that in most places, only components of the indicators are addressed to more explicitly identify what CT Competencies "look like" in the redesign of learning activities.

Kindergarten Reading

Ms. Fillion is a kindergarten teacher, returning for her second year in the classroom. She has been assigned an English language arts curriculum, but noticed several places where she can enhance student experience through inquiry and personal choice.

Ms. Fillion wants to use the CT Competencies to enrich her classroom experience, so she has decided to modify her lesson on story sequencing, while making sure to still cover the required objectives, including:

CCSS.ELA-LITERACY.RL.K.2: With prompting and support, retell familiar stories, including key details.

CCSS.ELA-LITERACY.L.K.1.D: Understand and use question words (interrogatives; e.g., who, what, where, when, why, how).

CCSS.ELA-LITERACY.SL.K.2: Confirm understanding of a text read aloud or information presented orally or through other media by asking and answering questions about key details and requesting clarification if something is not understood.

The original lesson calls for students to sit and listen to a familiar storybook and answer short, clarifying questions on certain pages. Afterward, there is a classroom discussion about the key story points. Following the discussion, students color a worksheet that helps them understand the "who, what, when, where, why and how" of the book.

Later that day or the next day, students are expected to retell the story from their own points of view, describing what they changed from the original and why. The lesson is relatively straightforward, but Ms. Fillion knows that she can fit in a couple of extra skills by arranging the lesson carefully.

Before she prepares her lesson, she finds a handful of CT Competencies that she finds interesting and useful and writes them down. Next, she lists actions she can take to achieve each of those competencies:

CT Competency	Idea
2a. Nurture a confident, competent and **positive identity around computing** for every student.	Every student approaches new learning opportunities differently. To build confidence and a positive identity, it will be important for teachers of young learners to establish that as a goal for all students.
4b. Design authentic learning activities that ask **students to leverage a design process** to solve problems with awareness of technical and human constraints and defend their design choices.	Have students take the story read in class and redesign it to reflect the way they would want it to go if they were in charge. Put students in pairs or small groups for brainstorming and reflection to explain their plan, then reflect on their choices.
4d. Create CS and CT learning environments that **value and encourage varied viewpoints**, student agency, creativity, engagement, joy and fun.	A fundamental tenet in CS and CT is solving open-ended problems. This helps lay the foundation for younger children to value different points of view that may lead to a more efficient solution.

After writing and reviewing ideas around competencies, Ms. Fillion recognizes that she can give students a few pointers on breaking the story into its main parts, using both discussion and a video from YouTube, then have students plan ideas for remixed stories with their partners. When it's time to put their stories together, they can execute them in a block-based story-centric programming environment, such as Scratch Jr., instead of merely drawing images. Her students' experience ranged from tentative to enthusiastic. During the lesson, she encouraged and guided student groups as well as making note of this in order to build confidence in her students. The class shared their stories and Ms. Fillion took this as a learning moment to discuss how the class expressed different points of view in their stories and why differing viewpoints can be valid.

By modifying her lesson in this way, Ms. Fillion is able to get in all of the requirements of the original lesson while also focusing on the CT Competencies that are meant to improve her classroom environment and build her students' exposure and facility with computational thinking.

Third-Grade Math

Mrs. Germaine is a veteran third-grade teacher, having taught in elementary schools for more than 15 years. She knows that students need positive math experiences in these foundational years to be confident and competent math learners.

Every year, a number of students struggle with rounding to the nearest 10, required for state tests and foundational knowledge in math. Having explored computational thinking a bit, she decided to redesign this unit to convey the concepts in an engaging new way. First, she reached out to a district tech coach to find out what online resources were available and get some curricular ideas to implement her unit. Mrs. Germaine also learned of a teacher, Mr. Lopez, at another school who was using an age-appropriate free platform for students to program interactive stories or games. He mentored her virtually on how to use the software and explored ideas for designing the learning activities so that the content was more engaging, fun and memorable.

Using backward design, she knew that she needed to build her activity to address this state standard:

- Use place value understanding to round whole numbers to the nearest 10 or 100.

In addition, she wanted to begin building her students' familiarity with these concepts:

- Decompose large numbers into their digit values (hundreds, tens and ones).
- Identify and fix bugs that prevent the game from representing the desired vision.
- Explain the choices and compromises made on the way to creating the game.

Mrs. Germaine created an activity where students worked in groups of three to build an online game with a theme of their choosing whereby students had to construct and decompose shapes made of unit squares.

Each student team would work together to identify a theme and each team member would identify two roles to play—designer, tester, timekeeper or subject matter expert.

Armed with her newly created exercise, she reviewed the CT Competencies to make sure that her classroom pedagogy reflected best practices for computational thinkers when it was time to deliver the lesson.

CT Competency	Idea
1a. Set professional learning goals to **explore and apply teaching strategies for integrating CT practices into learning activities in ways that enhance student learning of both the academic discipline and CS concepts.**	Learn integration strategies from other educators and apply them to math.
1c. **Leverage CT and CS experts**, resources and professional learning networks to continuously improve practice integrating CT across content areas.	Look beyond the pattern of "it's always been done this way" and try some advanced ideas involving CS/CT that colleagues successfully use in their classrooms.
3b. Apply effective **teaching strategies to support student collaboration around computing**, including **pair programming**, working in **varying team roles**, equitable workload distribution and project management.	Have students work in groups of three to support one another when exploring difficult ideas. Provide multiple role options so that students can try out different positions. As a lead learner, encourage students to rely on one another to problem-solve, rather than deferring to the teacher.
3c. **Plan collaboratively with other educators to create learning activities** that cross disciplines to strengthen student understanding of CT and CS concepts and transfer application of knowledge in new contexts.	Continue seeking out and developing relationships with educators of all subjects who are willing to explore age-appropriate CT and CS integration opportunities.

Mrs. Germaine found that her activity engaged students, but when they struggled with the programming, she encouraged them to keep trying and reminded them that they would know when they were on the right track because the game would work as it should. Students left satisfied and proud to complete their games so they could share them with their classmates.

Seventh-Grade Science

Mr. Davis teaches middle school science. For the last five years, he's been teaching about the water cycle, but this year he is switching over to Earth and human activity. As he researches the different sets of curricula, he wants to make sure he's as prepared as possible to incorporate CS and CT into his unit. Before it's time to make a choice, he takes a look at the CT Competencies to see which curricular options give him the most opportunity to practice these concepts.

The first thing he does is find a number of competencies that feel particularly meaningful, then he adds notes about qualities that he'll look for in lessons to help him achieve a handful of those items.

CT Competency	Notes
1a. Set professional learning goals to explore and apply teaching **strategies for integrating CT practices into learning activities** in ways that enhance student learning of both the academic discipline and CS concepts.	Analyze curriculum to find places where computational thinking practices can help achieve more integrated learning experiences; for example, having students collect data or find real data sets to use in projects.
2b. Construct and implement culturally relevant learning activities that address a diverse range of ethical, social and **cultural perspectives on computing** and highlight computing achievements from diverse role models and teams.	Reflect on the strengths and experiences of students; for example, encouraging English learners to use their language skills to design a tool to support non-native English speakers.
3a. Model and learn with students how to formulate computational solutions to problems and **how to give and receive actionable feedback**.	Consider opportunities to have students review and provide feedback on each other's projects; for example, by testing each other's apps and offering their perspectives as end users.
5b. Empower students to **select personally meaningful computational projects**.	Some of Mr. Davis' students lost their homes during the previous semester due to flooding. Choosing to focus his curriculum on natural disasters allows his students to engage in personally relevant projects.

Having made and reviewed his list, Mr. Davis chose a set of curriculum that included a module on collecting and modeling data about natural disasters, then allowed students to choose whether they would use these data to build an app intended to predict future disasters, help citizens in the midst of a natural disaster, or support neighborhoods trying to rebuild their physical spaces or their economy in the wake of a disaster.

10th-Grade Social Studies

Miss Jones and Mr. Bailey have been co-teaching 10th-grade history for three years. They recently went to a training on integrating CS and CT into other subjects and they are excited to bring what they've learned back to their classroom.

During the year, they generally teach a segment on the Industrial Revolution. They are required to hit all of the local standards associated with the topic, including:

U.S. II Standard 1.1: Students will assess how innovations in transportation, science, agriculture, manufacturing, technology, communication and marketing transformed America in the 19th and early 20th centuries.

U.S. II Standard 1.2: Students will explain the connections between the growth of industry, mining and agriculture, and the movement of people into and within the United States.

U.S. II Standard 1.3: Students will analyze the causal relationships between industrialization and the challenges faced by the growing working classes in urban settings.

U.S. II Standard 1.4: Students will use historical evidence to compare how industrial capitalist leaders used entrepreneurship, free markets and strategies to build their businesses.

With barely enough time in the year to incorporate all of the lessons that they already had planned, they knew that they would need to modify and combine a few elements in order for this experiment to be successful.

Fortunately, they had been grouped with other high school history teachers in their training, and together they had brainstormed some solutions. They had also made sure to share contact information to keep each other informed about what worked and what needed to be further refined.

Miss Jones and Mr. Bailey had agreed to work toward five CT Competencies in the first year and strive for five more in the following year. Given that plan, they wrote down their first set of competencies and made note of the ways that they intended to achieve them.

CT Competency	Notes
2d. Assess and manage classroom culture to drive **equitable student participation**, address exclusionary dynamics and **counter implicit bias**.	Identify learning/creation roles and include the transition of roles in multiple projects. Model and discuss the importance of words/terms/pronouns choice when discussing technical or project team roles for class and how the students can apply this in their lives.
4a. Design CT activities where data can be obtained, **analyzed** and represented to support problem-solving and learning in other content areas.	Design this unit so students access data on incomes and wages surrounding the revolution, use computing tools to analyze the data and make inferences about what affected incomes and wages, and make a prediction based on variables that would have increased them.
5c. **Use a variety of instructional approaches** to help students frame problems in ways that can be represented as computational steps or algorithms to be performed by a computer.	They decided to set each of the three projects for the year in a different medium. Give students the opportunity to create small digital products in the beginning and work up to a larger app-based project. Move progressively from instruction-based learning toward inquiry-based learning.
5d. Establish criteria for evaluating CT practices and content learning that use a variety of formative and alternative assessments to enable students to **demonstrate their understanding of age-appropriate CS and CT vocabulary**, practices and concepts.	Ask students to self-assess their CT skills to help reinforce their definitions. Allow students to choose their computational artifact and use a rubric to evaluate how they design solutions that are user-centered. Have students assess each other's projects before they are turned in to highlight areas of CT and CS done correctly and incorrectly.

By combining these with the ideas that they picked up at training, Miss Jones and Mr. Bailey decided that they would start adopting competencies around major projects, with the intention of broadening the scope to include all activities once they became more comfortable.

Getting Started
With the CT Competencies

A Simple Pathway

We recognize that change takes time. Instead of seeing the CT Competencies as extra hoops to jump through, we invite you to treat them as personal goals that help provide benchmarks for your role in your classroom's digital-age journey, and as a guide to help you recognize where you may already be using CT practices in your classroom. If your personal pedagogical style is already intentionally equitable, engaging, personalized and highlighted by your own lead learner moments, then you are likely already incorporating these competencies at some level. If, on the other hand, none of these standards feel like they mesh well with your classroom environment, we encourage you to take a look at your curricular and pedagogical choices to find places where you can stretch your practice and enhance your students' learning experience with CT.

Once you have decided that the CT Competencies journey is a trip worth taking, it's time to break the process into steps.

1. Reflect

Develop a plan to first test the waters, then make a splash! Looking at the CT Competencies, can any of them enhance your teaching practice to meet the goals or address the challenges you outlined in step one?

a. What can you do to immediately add impact (including social, creative or environmental) to your teaching? Find an indicator that can help you with that goal.

b. How can you help your students think about who they are, what they stand for and how they can affect their community? Find an indicator that can help you with that goal.

c. How can you modify your current prep process to include more moments where you are learning along with your students instead of merely teaching them? Find an indicator that can help you with that goal.

d. What opportunities are there to share your successes and techniques with your colleagues? Find an indicator that can help you with that goal.

e. Are there any assignments, projects or assessments for your classes that could be enhanced by the inclusion of CS/CT? Itemize the types of computer science tools that might be fun to integrate. Find an indicator that can help you with that goal.

> Example tools include integrated development environments (IDEs) that help you code apps for smartphones or other devices, drag-and-drop platforms for home assistants like Alexa and programming interfaces for simple hardware like the micro:bit.

f. Look at the remaining CT Competencies. Do any of them speak to you as being particularly important? What reflections would they help you enhance? Weave the indicators together with the reflection and see what kind of classroom activity ideas come of it.

g. Finally, look at any of the CT Competencies that are left over. Do any of them feel irrelevant? Why do you think that is? Is there something about the underlying intention of those standards that will not work for your classroom? How would you modify them to be actionable for you and your students? Use those modifications to complete your plan.

2. Execute

We don't expect you to act on all of these competencies immediately—it's OK to think of this as a growth pathway! The goal is to figure out what you can do to start making a positive change, then build on that experience until you create the most meaningful and lasting CT learning experiences with your students.

a. Using the box below, identify two or three competencies that you can implement in the classroom this week.
b. Identify two or three more that you believe you can fit in by the end of the term.
c. Are there two or three more that you can work in later in the school year?
d. Which CT Competencies do you think you can reach next school year, with the right amount of planning and collaboration with fellow educators?

Immediately	Within This Term	Within This School Year	By Next School Year

3. Revise

As your learning grows, you will realize that your understanding deepens and you can revise your first attempts at redesigning a learning activity. Use these prompts to review, reflect and revise learning activities:

a. Check-in with yourself a week into the process. Was anything easier or more difficult than expected? Revise your plan based on your experience and see if there are any additional standards that can be integrated into the term.
b. Revisit your plan again at the end of the term. What have you learned? Was anything easier or more difficult than expected? Revise your plan based on your experience and see if there are any additional competencies that can be integrated into your practice throughout the year.
c. Look at your plan again at the end of the year and see if your lens has shifted at all. Who can you work with to meaningfully integrate these CT Competencies into your educational experience next year?
d. Make a new plan for next school year, based on a new series of answers to your previous reflection questions. Include a goal around sharing your experience with other educators to receive feedback from peers and provide encouragement to others.

It's no coincidence that the steps provided closely mirror the elements of design thinking. To encourage continuous improvement, the pathway is defined as a circular list of steps that leads from reflecting → planning → executing → reflecting/revising → executing → reflecting/revising and so on until you've ended up with a classroom, strengthened by computational thinking, that works for you and your students.

When building your plan, feel free to include additional standards in the process to keep your lessons holistic, interdisciplinary and connected. We'll give you an idea of how the CT Competencies from ISTE blend with other digital age standards in the following section.

The Connected Landscape

Student learning is most powerful when multiple areas converge to form a coherent, meaningful and relevant experience. In the section that follows, we will explain how the ISTE Standards for Educators: Computational Thinking Competencies fit in the larger landscape of standards and suggestions for their use.

ISTE—The Big Picture

All of the principles of great education still hold true when incorporating computer science and/or computational thinking into your curriculum. The CT Competencies were designed to enhance the ISTE Standards for Educators (iste.org/standards/for-educators) and deepen student learning across academic areas.

To understand how these two sets of educator standards might work together, let's dive into a couple of specific recommendations.

The first ISTE Standard for Educators indicator (1a) is:

> **Set professional learning goals to explore and apply pedagogical approaches made possible by technology and reflect on their effectiveness.**

and you can imagine that might pair well with 1b. in the CT Competency:

> **Develop a foundational knowledge of pedagogies and assessment strategies that support the development of deep and aligned student learning of CS concepts and computational thinking practices.**

The two can definitely be done separately, but think of how much more powerful they become together!

Similarly, ISTE Standards for Educators indicator 3a:

> **Create experiences for learners to make positive, socially responsible contributions and exhibit empathetic behavior online that build relationships and community.**

could work very well with CT Competency 6f:

> **Facilitate critical examination of implicit bias and stereotyping in interactions, product design and development methods.**

Can you imagine the kinds of changemakers that our classrooms would foster if we intentionally worked to observe the inequities around us and helped students do something about it?

These standards are meant to be ingredients in your own recipe algorithm, allowing you to craft experiences for your classroom that create learners who are aware and empowered to use the power of computing for problem-solving, creative expression and more! Take a quick look at the two sets of standards yourself. Can you make any pairings that excite you? Check out the full set of ISTE Standards for Educators and try to create your own custom blends!

ISTE Standards for Educators

The ISTE Standards for Educators are your road map to helping students become empowered learners. These standards will deepen your practice, promote collaboration with peers, challenge you to rethink traditional approaches and prepare students to drive their own learning.

Empowered Professional

1. Learner

Educators continually improve their practice by learning from and with others and exploring proven and promising practices that leverage technology to improve student learning. Educators:

a. Set professional learning goals to explore and apply pedagogical approaches made possible by technology and reflect on their effectiveness.

b. Pursue professional interests by creating and actively participating in local and global learning networks.

c. Stay current with research that supports improved student learning outcomes, including findings from the learning sciences.

2. Leader

Educators seek out opportunities for leadership to support student empowerment and success and to improve teaching and learning. Educators:

a. Shape, advance and accelerate a shared vision for empowered learning with technology by engaging with education stakeholders.

b. Advocate for equitable access to educational technology, digital content and learning opportunities to meet the diverse needs of all students.

c. Model for colleagues the identification, exploration, evaluation, curation and adoption of new digital resources and tools for learning.

3. Citizen

Educators inspire students to positively contribute to and responsibly participate in the digital world. Educators:

a. Create experiences for learners to make positive, socially responsible contributions and exhibit empathetic behavior online that build relationships and community.

b. Establish a learning culture that promotes curiosity and critical examination of online resources and fosters digital literacy and media fluency.

c. Mentor students in safe, legal and ethical practices with digital tools and the protection of intellectual rights and property.

d. Model and promote management of personal data and digital identity and protect student data privacy.

4. Collaborator

Educators dedicate time to collaborate with both colleagues and students to improve practice, discover and share resources and ideas, and solve problems. Educators:

a. Dedicate planning time to collaborate with colleagues to create authentic learning experiences that leverage technology.

b. Collaborate and learn with students to discover and use new digital resources and diagnose and troubleshoot technology issues.

c. Use collaborative tools to expand students' authentic, real-world learning experiences by engaging virtually with experts, teams and students, locally and globally.

d. Demonstrate cultural competency when communicating with students, parents and colleagues and interact with them as collaborators in student learning.

5. Designer

Educators design authentic, learner-driven activities and environments that recognize and accommodate learner variability. Educators:

a. Use technology to create, adapt and personalize learning experiences that foster independent learning and accommodate learner differences and needs.

b. Design authentic learning activities that align with content area standards and use digital tools and resources to maximize active, deep learning.

c. Explore and apply instructional design principles to create innovative digital learning environments that engage and support learning.

6. Facilitator

Educators facilitate learning with technology to support student achievement of the 2016 ISTE Standards for Students. Educators:

a. Foster a culture where students take ownership of their learning goals and outcomes in both independent and group settings.

b. Manage the use of technology and student learning strategies in digital platforms, virtual environments, hands-on makerspaces or in the field.

c. Create learning opportunities that challenge students to use a design process and computational thinking to innovate and solve problems.

d. Model and nurture creativity and creative expression to communicate ideas, knowledge or connections.

7. Analyst

Educators understand and use data to drive their instruction and support students in achieving their learning goals. Educators:

a. Provide alternative ways for students to demonstrate competency and reflect on their learning using technology.

b. Use technology to design and implement a variety of formative and summative assessments that accommodate learner needs, provide timely feedback to students and inform instruction.

c. Use assessment data to guide progress and communicate with students, parents and education stakeholders to build student self-direction.

Other Digital Age Standards

ISTE recognizes that we are not alone in the pursuit of formative CS and CT opportunities that are both engaging and accessible for all students. Our vision has been made stronger because of deep collaboration with organizations like CSTA, CSforALL and members of the K–12 CS Framework Committee, which share our belief that a strong foundation in CS and CT will empower students to succeed in all academic areas.

How These Resources Relate

The K–12 CS Framework, the CSTA Standards (for students) and the ISTE Standards for Educators: Computational Thinking Competencies (for teachers) work together as part of an ecosystem of resources that supports students, educators and leaders to craft rigorous and equitable CS learning opportunities:

- **The CS K–12 Framework** is a high-level guide for states, districts and organizations that represents the essential ideas in computer science for all students. This document was written in collaboration with many leading experts in CS/CT/technology education and was meant to provide an organizing structure and guidance for implementing computer science education.

- **The CSTA K–12 Computer Science Standards** are specific goals, grouped by grade band, that articulate in detail a core set of learning objectives for students to provide the foundation for a complete computer science curriculum and its implementation at the K–12 level.

- **The CT Competencies** are core practices for teachers of all grades that outline the knowledge, skills and dispositions for integrating computational thinking across content areas, and empower students to innovate and solve problems through computing. They were designed to ensure students receive a holistic, equitable CS education.

Helpful Resources

We hope that you have a clearer picture of why CT matters for every educator and have received a few ideas for where to start. There is a universe of online resources and support dedicated to CS and CT education! However, we know that having too many choices can sometimes be just as frustrating as having too few!

To help guide your lesson planning, we have outlined a few of our favorite resources for adding CS and/or CT to your lesson plans. If you need quick access to our favorites in the future, please bookmark iste.org/computer-science.

Resources for Adding Computer Science

CS Unplugged: University of Canterbury, New Zealand

CS Unplugged is a collection of free learning activities that teach computer science through engaging games and puzzles that use cards, string, crayons and lots of running around.

(https://classic.csunplugged.org)

CAS Barefoot Computing: Supported by BT

Created by a team of practicing computing teachers, these quality, cross-curricular activities help primary teachers deliver the computing curriculum in engaging and practical ways.

(https://barefootcas.org.uk)

Code.org

Code.org provides the leading curriculum for K–12 computer science in the largest school districts in the United States. Code.org also organizes the annual Hour of Code campaign, which has engaged 10% of all students in the world.

(https://code.org)

No Fear Coding: ISTE

No-Fear Coding shows K–5 educators how to bring coding into their curriculum by embedding computational thinking skills into activities for every content area. At the same time, embedding these skills helps students prepare for coding in the middle grades as they build their knowledge.

(http://bit.ly/NoFearBook)

Creative Coding: ISTE

This book helps classroom teachers in several core content areas develop activities and projects to encourage computational thinking and coding skills, and to build bridges between those skills and practice.

(http://bit.ly/CreativeCodingJosh)

Resources for Integrating Computational Thinking

Introduction to Computational Thinking for Every Educator: ISTE

Developed with support from Google, this course will provide you with a clear definition of CT, explain how it differs from computer science and unpack how it can be integrated into a variety of subject areas. You'll increase your awareness of CT, experiment with examples of CT-integrated activities for the subject areas you teach and create a plan to integrate CT into your own curricula.

(https://www.iste.org/learn/iste-u/computational-thinking)

Computational Thinking and Coding for Every Student: Corwin

Our students are avid users and consumers of technology. Isn't it time that they see themselves as the next technological innovators, too? Computational Thinking and Coding for Every Student is the beginner's guide for K–12 educators who want to learn to integrate the basics of computer science into their curriculum.

(http://bit.ly/CTandCoding)

Computational Thinking Resource Site: ISTE

Computer science is more than just coding. Thinking like a computer scientist involves being creative and thinking collaboratively about a problem in order to solve it.

(http://bit.ly/CTbyISTE)